We dedicate this book to everyone who wants to explore the potential of what living miracles can achieve.

Thank you to each of our children: Blake, Maeve and Matty, for inspiring us and helping us grow daily.

Am I A Sheep?
The Courage of Individualism

Dr. Kristin Heins, ND
& Marc Finkelstein

We are all born different,
and the ways are so many.

Things like skin, hair,
our likes, and being funny.

Being unique is special and something to celebrate.

But sometimes we don't,
 we're afraid to be great.

Sheep are the same, we can't tell them apart.

They move in a herd, and don't follow their hearts.

Like you, they're all different

but they hide in their fleece.

With the hopes and desires they wish

to release.

So they act like the others and don't even blink.

There's safety in being the same, so they think.

They "baa" and they graze, each one is a clone.

They are all just so scared of being alone.

Some groups ignore others

who are not like them too.

Missing out on neat zebras,

cool cats, kangaroos.

It is so very boring to live like a sheep.

That's why we count them when falling asleep.

Your friends may behave in ways you dislike.

They may push you to like the things that they like.

If you can't be yourself,

perhaps best take a hike.

Life is not fun when we act like somebody else.

True joy can be found

just by being yourself.

When you are yourself,

you feel all of your splendour.

Your radiance,

your being, the ways you are tender.

You are loved and adored for all that's inside.

People are not perfect,

you've got nothing to hide.

So be BRAVE and be **bold**

don't be a sheep.

Be your true self,

it's not a big leap.

Children greatly rely on socialization and the media as they develop self identity, values, and normative behavioural responses. Many years can be spent in discord and struggle before children discover the freedom that can exist when finding and acting their true selves.

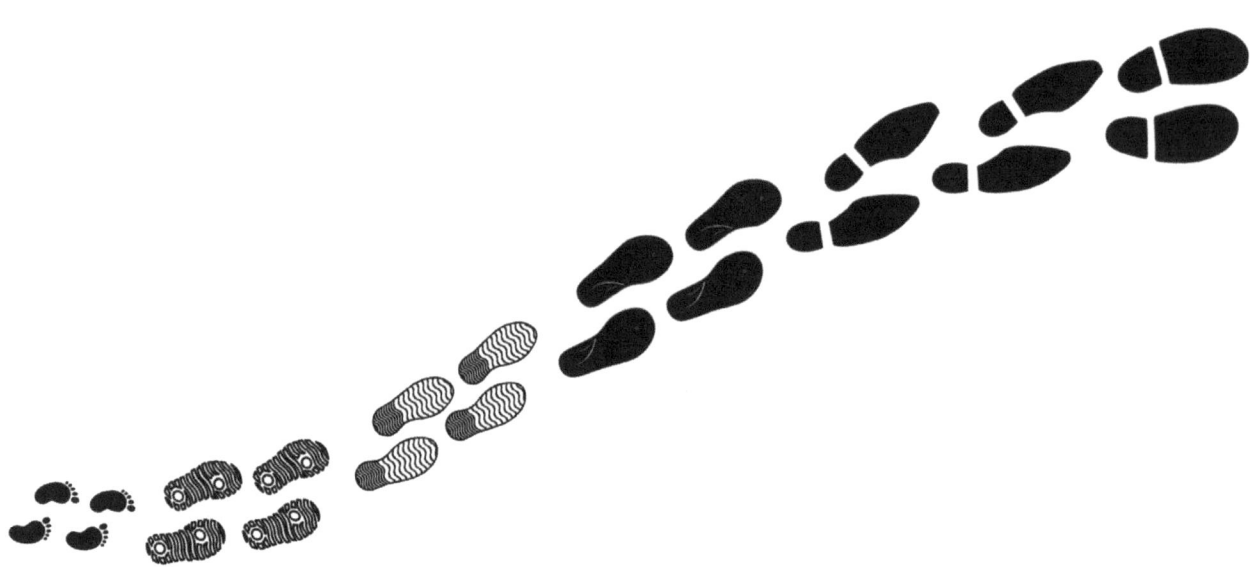

Through this series, and with the help of their caregivers and educators, children can more easily understand authenticity and personal mastery, both introspectively and within the world around them.

Kristin is a naturopathic doctor who has been studying humanistic and relational psychotherapy for the past decade and currently works under clinical supervision.

Marc is a PhD (candidate) in Decision Science, author and specialist in behavioural science.

Both authors are parents, and are passionate about nurturing the life skills necessary for children (and their caregivers) to bravely be the people they are.

Many thanks to the creative team for helping to bring these books to life.

© 2017 Marc Finkelstein & Kristin Heins

All rights reserved. This book or parts thereof may not be reproduced in any form, stored in any retrieval system, or transmitted in any form by any means—electronic, mechanical, photocopy, recording, or otherwise—without prior written permission of the publisher, except as provided by law. For permission requests, write to the publisher, at the address below.

Published worldwide by
Masala Enterprises Limited
1400 - 52 Lawrence Avenue West
Toronto, ON M5M 1A4

www.masalaenterprises.ca

For information about purchasing in bulk, educational needs, professional needs, or other special orders, contact Masala Enterprises at 1-866-999-2907 or sales@masalaenterprises.ca.

Book series information:
www.WhoAmIBooks.ca

Hardcover: 978-1-7752179-3-0 | Paperback: 978-1-7752179-4-7 | eBook: 978-1-7752179-5-4

www.ingramcontent.com/pod-product-compliance
Lightning Source LLC
Chambersburg PA
CBHW041715160426
43209CB00018B/1844